Things I Don't Want To Talk About

Things I Don't Want To Talk About

Poems by Carolyn Hill-Bjerke

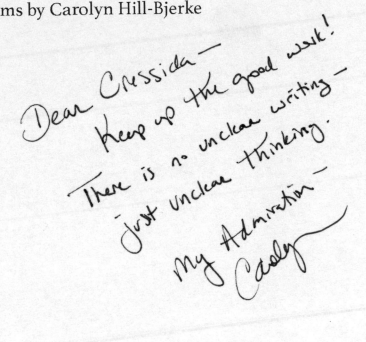

Dear Cressida —
Keep up the good work!
There is no unclear writing —
just unclear thinking.

My Admiration —
Carolyn

Cover art and layout by Wayne Braino Bjerke

Published by Word Poetry
P.O. Box 541106
Cincinnati, OH 45254-1106

ISBN: 9781625491701

Poetry Editor: Kevin Walzer
Business Editor: Lori Jareo

Visit us on the web at
www.wordpoetrybooks.com

for my husband, Wayne

Poetry: the best words in the best order.
—*Samuel Taylor Coleridge*

Table of Contents

III

Acknowledgements

Upon My Lover's Departure   *Mississippi Review* 2007

Pan Am Flight 103   *Fish Stories*

Lot's Wife   *Paper Street Press*
                                    Nominated for a Pushcart Prize

The Renewal of 4M   *Atlanta Review* 2003

As a Transgression of Divine Law   Issue 12 *Podium*
                                    (online magazine 92nd Street Y)

Loss
Crisis
Misplaced Ceremony   *Coachella Review* Summer 2014

Willow Me   Short film directed by Becky Razzell,
                                    Fall 2013

Things I Don't Want To Talk About

I

Willow Me

I stand in the ground overlooking the graves.
I look over the dead. My friends are tombstones.
My leaves decorate their ledges.

My roots are tough and tenacious.
I smelled the earth long ago.
Now my head brushes the clouds.

I cast shadows on those who walk beneath me.
They remember seeing me and sometimes
Carve themselves into my base.

My rings grow wider as I witness more holes.
Everyone finds me—
But I have no recollection of me as a sapling.
I don't remember the water or love.
But I do know the sun took time to nourish me.

I stand alone.
Branches have sprouted and grown.
Some say I took root from a broken branch
from another tree now long gone.
My roots formed without supervision.

I am strong and one day, if I let you,
you may climb into me.

Life Song

First, I felt the whole falling to pieces in my sea.
Life hit me so hard, I fell out of my head –
then the mountain fell on top of me.

I found myself hiding in a cave receiving
cold water freezing the shards of myself now dead.
First, I felt the whole falling to pieces in my sea.

I stepped on a fragment of myself freed
and reached for the slippery piece of dread—
then the mountain fell on top of me.

Before the envelope arrived, I thought I'd be
who I was – not what my unchosen past said.
First, I felt the whole falling to pieces in my sea.

As I swallowed my water, I count the three
branches that can save me. Reach, please, really !
Then the mountain fell on top of me.

I lifted the veil covering your eyes only to see
who carried a bag heavier—you or me.
First, I felt the whole falling to pieces in my sea.
Then the mountain fell on top of me.

Untethered

My foot slipped and I fell off of my world.
The celestial clouds looked like tangible cliffs
that perhaps I could navigate with a few fingers
but the air just jetted between my fingers.

I slide out of my body and floated towards the black
of my unconscious. Untethered, I have drifted away
from grocery lists, subway stops, and urgent emails.
Just trying to make myself a cup of tea takes two hours.

Time stops having actual meaning. I watch events happen.
I do not participate. The memory of you is not enough
to bring my soul back into my reality so I feel the soil.
There are no smells. Just cold. Leave a message, please.

Breath is real when my new reality seems like fractured images.
I hear myself draw in existence as I feel myself surrounded by
souls who need introductions but tell me they have known me
for decades. Can someone introduce me? I no longer recognize
myself.

Upon My Lover's Departure

for Canto V of the Inferno

I was lying face down
the sheets still warm
with your wretchedness when
my window burst open in a shout—
one being with two heads
twirled about me as I realized
that these dead two were one.

"You can't trust them," Francesca said.
Paolo looked out the window at a bird
rather than at me curled in my bed. "I will
show you eternal embrace without devotion."
Francesca gazed down at her intertwined
torso and stroked love's remains. Paolo sighed.
"Just don't read too much," he said. "You would
be surprised by the damage God can allow words."

Crushed

Find me.
Find my body in a state of collapse.
The information fell on top of my body
and crushed me through the circles
past the Lethe into a place of thorns
where my body now lies as I struggle
to remember the memory of before.

Powerless against the weight of myself
the thorns prick my skin with such
intensity that it almost feels good.
Like the adrenaline rush of a tattoo.
I forget to feel myself. I just accept
this new state of being.
There is no before.
Just after.

First

I was standing in the dusty market. People were selling
olives, dried dates, oils, and fabric. My father came towards
me dressed in a light colored robe. He held a walking stick.

The dirty young face appeared before me and as soon as I
saw it—the market disappeared. There was only her.
She ran from me. I wanted to follow her, but my father
yelled my name. He told me that was not what I am here for.

My father lead me through the market and out of the city
towards the river. When we got to the riverbank he pointed
at the flowing river and instructed me to look into it.
"This is your life," he said.

The girl with the dirty face appeared on the other side of
the bank. "Mother," she said. "I am here to tell you that I am ok."
The young girl was about five years old—the same age as my
daughter in this life. The girl had dirt caked on her face.
She explained that her face was dirty because she was in the
stable with me when I died. She was my first daughter.

Her name was Nala. She wanted me to know that her life was good.
She was ok. She married well and had a happy life. I could stop
looking for her now. My soul spent centuries looking for Nala's spirit.
My body expelled the last fetus that tried to take up residence
because my soul would not take another being. It had to be Nala.

And now, it doesn't. I understand. She was ok. I can stop looking.
I can leave her in the past and stop trying to bring her into this world.
She lived. It's over. My soul can move on and bring someone else
into my body, into my world, into my life.

Our Challenges

Oh, Proust.
I too planned and abandoned many literary undertakings
due to a lack of artistic parental support. How were we
to know in our youth that their wrongs can still be right?
Your father practiced medicine to treat the ill. For me,
it was my mother. She was the doctor. I know you'd be impressed
by this. In fact, I have often considered how my introspection
with the pen mirrored her daily delve into the hidden lives of others,
as she was a psychiatrist. But, I know how difficult it is to defend
a life in literature when the parents in question refuse to dignify literature
with the title "career." Well, we both took to the sheets and surrounded
ourselves with our books and other artists. Both of us have taken
to scratching along our thoughts in masked disguise, the beauty of
words is the ability to hide ourselves in plain sight and extract memories
so they do not have to live within us and constantly keep us awake.

Self Portrait

Come past this entrance.
Let me show you myself
alone in a crib. I lay on
foster blankets while
my papers shuffle and land
before a pile of abandon wombs.
Which one will I fill?
I die as a bastard
and resurrect myself
as a newborn.

In my next life, I am married and pregnant
when my body laughed at me. The sharp
egg ripped me right into surgery. Now
I move on with a barren womb, just like
the paper mother I was given.

The last time I died, I was rushing downtown
In a blizzard of "to dos." I arrived so close to chaos
that I didn't even see the steel gashes melting.
A simple shouted direction saved me as
soul dust choked those just South of me.

Here we are. Lowered into the depths
of my deaths. Each one leaving this hole
wider. It's slick and I have to close
my eyes. It's too hard to watch yourself
projected on the big screen. Each move
seems so fake. I have repeated this process
so many times that I think I know how
to live between worlds.

In the Garden of My Birth

The priest told me I could stop looking
under the stones where I thought you were hiding.
Onion paper and typewriters blurred us from each other,
and forced me into this existence with the other mother.
Jesus moved his stone, but I cannot even find mine
in order to move it. I can see, but the myths make me blind.
My eyes know they have seen you, but I cannot recall
the fall of your hair or shape of your face. I was too small.
My hair was the same black as my assumed father.
You did not see that hair fall out and grow back mother blonde.
The imprints of you float trapped in my mind. I must have felt
your hugs through the rough hospital blanket as love can melt.
Oh, why did you leave me, I asked head in hand -- decade after decade.
Now, the papers surfaced with their typewritten certainty and my price paid,
it was revealed that you had been cast away to the institutions
and it was I who left you. I was taken from you as a solution
by the powerful pens. No matter how much I search within myself –
I am not going to find that stone. Maybe it never existed. Or, if
I manage to stumble upon it, I will find a stone covered with
the graffiti of your name scrawled and faded, memory and myth.

Walking Alone

I try not to look over my shoulder
when I'm walking down the street.
I fear one day, some crazy woman
will tap my shoulder and tell me

she's my mother. And then what do I do?
Take her home and make soup,
introduce her to my husband
and let her pet my dog? By why

did she leave me nearly 30 years ago?
I know my father was not there
when I was born. She was alone.
I have struggled for years to know myself—

And now that I think I do, I can't let some nut
crack open the vision I have created—
the one behind the window
I can't open or see through.

I can't break it, but I know it's there.
When I'm walking down Third Avenue—
I look straight ahead, walk as fast as I can
to avoid the woman behind me.

Diving

I went up to the heavens
and found a piece of my soul unarchived,
hiding in a pile of severed feathers.

Once I saw myself, this shard of soul
raised its infant head from the feathers
and looked out past the void of myself.

The piece of my soul then leapt
from the nest of dead limbs while
the Archangel Michael awaited my approach.

A line of angels on the right were totally white.
A line of angels on the left were totally black.
The new part of my soul, now retrieved, walked with Michael—

And after he escorted this virgin piece of myself
past the messengers—some known, some unknown—
it dove into the skin of my old soul and blew it apart—

so that pieces of myself scattered
then gathered with the beauty of a stained
glass window which illuminates light in shadows.

Moon Beams

After I was found, I spent a few days examining
the broken years I was misplaced in another dwelling.
In the past, every time curiosity rose to my surface,
I hit it back down with a hammer of can't, not, never.

Someone turned me in. Someone turned his back.
Someone left her while she was trying to keep me.
Then I was lost in a dark confusion that covered itself
in paper so no one who knew about me could find me.

I went on.
I grew.
Never you nor of you I knew.
Until now.

The moon rose and looked across the map
to see us; separated by land, not blood—
separated by those papers not wire or waves.
Memory of my dawn does not exist.

But the moon remembered me and it decided to
help me see. Sunlight of day kept my eyes too full.
You searched but forgot to look a few streets away.
We did not have names. But we have eyes that match.

The moon shone bright so I could see in the dark
and run my fingers along the paper I was given that
had your name embossed on it. The beams were like x-rays
showing me parts of myself never before seen by anyone.

Loss

after Ezra Pound

Loss knows me,
knows my body
knows my name
remembers my face
and constantly
picks me out of a crowd.

Pan Am Flight 103

The smiling face behind
the ticket counter at Heathrow
wished me a happy
flight home.

My mother has red hair—
           I am from New Jersey—

After my first kiss, Jimmy held
my head
beneath the pool water.
I jumped to gasp for the summer air
and broke my tooth.
(I didn't smile for a year.)

Last weekend I bought
that Spanish leather wallet
for my father.

I didn't even want to go home—

Thick damp air strong with
cigarette smoke and baked potatoes
at Camden Market.
Vendors sold black jeans
—a Grateful Dead tape from 1974—
I loved to look over the canal
that divided the shoppers and the stalls,
smoking a Silk Cut from a white and purple box.

I saw myself
        in a mirror
        with pink hair and black nail polish.

I read every single Jane Austen novel
        and walked along Emma's gossip
        in the footpaths of Southern England.
A lover betrayed me, I became the other woman.

Now
my red duffle bag
        spills
across the earth
the photos I took
by the Trevi fountain in Rome...
My feet are cold.

I want to hold my dog—
bury my nose in his warm fur
it smells like...

Describing a Ghost

I think I have seen you before.
Were you once made of lye? or stone ? or wood?
No, always flesh. Hm.
I can't seem to make out your face.

It's as if God was in the middle of creating someone,
and took a phone call and forgot what he was doing.
He was distracted because Satan told him that he
had been walking up and down the earth.

When God turned around you sauntered away,
roaming around on your own with no direction,
just evanescent. It's as if freedom confused you,
so you chose the purgatory of our temporal earth.

I want you to know that I exist here and I feel you.
Physicality and memory may be gone, but you still
have a presence that brushes against me like a cat
across my ankle, creating chills to tell me someone

touched me.

Preservation

Walking through the streets of Liverpool
to interview the Director of Housing, I
came across an empty church so charred
it looked like the tip of a burnt match.

It seemed so black and so brittle
a small breeze could extinguish it.

When I arrived at the Office of Housing
and Social Services, I greeted the Director,
took my tea, and asked how recently the fire
had destroyed their church down the street.

Activity buzzing around the office suddenly
stopped as his co-workers awaited the answer.

The director laughed as he explained: the church
was a memorial to those who had died
in the bombing of England during WWII,
and how "very American" of me to think it recent.

Unfinished Studies

After I lost myself, I stumbled upon that stone altar
I created for you years ago in a sloppy corner of my mind where
we wobbled on London cobblestone streets— both of us equally
hazy with our pint-minds. We poured our feelings into each other
like the lager from the taps. The fast breath of youth created our thirst.

It had taken me a month to work up the gumption to speak to you
beyond my half pint of lager order at the Intrepid Fox pub on
Wardour Street.
You filled my eyes with black leather while The Damned filled my
ears with roses.
I sat on that piano bench watching the purple hair and piercings of
the punks go by.
Once, the girl in front of me almost passed out from doing whip-its.
I had pink hair.

The other American girls I was studying with refused to attend my
rebellion in Soho. I was left alone in the flashing Peep Show lights. I
would drink with you in the Dive Bar when you weren't working at the
Fox. You asked to meet my parents. Although a punk rocker, you were
still an English gentleman. We dined in Chinatown.
I smoked through dinner as I forgot words, while you proposed to
my mother.

My memory forms the imagination of you. But, I still have the pictures
to prove
I was in your flat and in your bedroom. A photo of you sat on my desk
for years. When I wrote to you last week to remind you it had been
twenty-five years since

I sat in the West End Police Station until 3 a.m. waiting for you, you wrote me right back— you had just thought of that night. Love as always, Mick. Big sigh

The shared history of our youth always brings us back to together. Remember the time we made out in the Dive Bar and we thought we'd be thrown out? You loved my American accent, which I always forgot I had. We were exotic to each other.
I worship those passions you taught me and lay here on the stones of you I created drugged with nostalgia and wondering if any of this past was real or just fabricated.

Understanding The Philosopher's Marker

Now that we know change,
we can verify Aristotle's definition
of time which tells us that time
is the numbering of change
according to before and after.

Words

after Philip Larkin

What are words for?
Words are where we live.
They exist, they wake us,
syllable by syllable.
Words are to be happy in:
where else can poets live but words?

Ah, answering that question
just brings a poet closer and closer
to picking up a brush
and simply illustrating the colors of the world.

II

Unborn

I wonder why it took me so long
to see you there. You were on my desk
along with the paper clips and Post-It notes,
which listed all of the things I needed to do.

Maybe it was because you were covered
with appointments and unwatched dvds. Maybe it
was because I did not want to see you, feel you.

But I see you now.
I have to pick you up.
and to hug you—
and soak my shirt with your smell.

I have folded and tucked you inside.
We breathe together. I feel your
movements and if I had allowed
myself to listen more carefully
for the sound of the heartbeats, I
would have wanted you sooner.

The Office Visit

I was walking towards the coat closet
after my appointment. I saw the nurse
who had her daughter in June. She smiled
as I had seen her so often during her
last trimester. She handed me my bill.

"So how's your baby?" she asked.
I pressed my pen down into my
check book and without looking up
I said, "Thanks for asking,
I had a miscarriage."

Ruptures

I was checking her as a doctor would;
trying not to look like a fellow patient.
My disaster was dwarfed by hers.
Shock closed both our eyes—
afraid to look at the results
of explosions that struck each
of us in the lower extremities.

Someone threw planes like darts
into her womb and killed the twins.
Mine was more like a ruptured
water pipe, drowning me with myself.
Her dust and my liquid created
quite a slick mud that fall:
everyone near us lost footing.

The last couple of weeks that September
we both lolled our heads on a pillow
of surrealism; reality blurred by
painkillers. Everyone watched, weighed,
monitored our movements and pulse.
The cycle of loss left us barren as
we prepared to stand alone again.

Witness to the Despondent

I was in the grocery store check out line
catching up on the latest gossip in *Star*
when I watched a couple enter the store
with their daughter. For a moment, I thought
she was in a big stroller until I realized that
she was probably nine or ten years old.

The apparatus she rode in was a complicated
wheelchair intended to cushion her bent limbs.
Her hair was pushed back in a clip her mother
must have fixed for her. She had a blanket
wrapping her legs against the chill.

The Father pushed the wheelchair. The Mother
silently hurried towards an aisle to retrieve
several food items as if this detour into
the mundane lives of we supermarket shoppers
was alien territory and unpleasant at that.

I noticed a small carton of Horizon Organic
Chocolate milk with a skinny red straw
sitting in the daughter's lap. Just as I was
about to smile, the young girl opened her mouth
and out flew the ingested milk.

My quest to the cashier seemed insignificant
as my maternal instincts leapt into my foot
which moved to rush over to the father. But,
before I could even move, the mother poked
her head out of the frozen food aisle and gave

a nod. The defeated father wheels his daughter
quickly out of the store.

I could see him from where my cashier dragged
applesauce for my own daughter over the scanner.
I kept an eye on the father standing outside.
He had a look and dullness to his eyes that
I can only attribute to the length and intensity
of whatever ailed his daughter. It wasn't just
the chocolate milk incident.

I wanted to leave my own silly supermarket
selection on the moving conveyer belt and
rush out to that sidewalk. I wanted to help
that father clean up the daughter. I wanted to tell
him that I knew how he felt as my own toddler
had just spent the last five days wretching in a
portable crib in a beachfront hotel room in Miami
while it rained and hailed there for the first time in months.

But I couldn't do it.
The mother had walked to the check out aisle
next to me. I could smell the sadness that
cloaked this family in a triangle of the
incurable. No one knew how they felt.
No one had read the script to their drama.
Each page was being written day by day.
No words providing the comfort sought.
My only alternative was to pick up the pen
and try for compassion.

Crisis

It was a crisis.
I was a crisis.
I am good in a crisis.
The crisis ruined lives.
What is a crisis?
It is a stage in a sequence of events
at which the trend of all future
events, for better or worse is determined.

My crisis divided people.
I was the crisis.
A crisis ruins people.
As a crisis, I caused
my mother to fall to pieces
in white beds while I waited
in an orphanage, a foster home,
then away from her.

I have not found her
to stroke her head
after the crisis of myself.
They say she might have
survived the crisis if
I had died. Maybe I am
dead. I am still in crisis.

Lot's Wife

And as she trailed her co-workers
down the labyrinth of stairs
for minutes that seemed like days,
she shed some tears thinking

of her college diploma on the wall,
her beagle salt & pepper shakers,
her first child's finger painting—
not to mention the coffee station

where she stole a kiss last month
from the young marketing manager—
all abandoned during that journey
from sky views into the depths:

sirens and fire. When she reached
the lobby, clutching her Kate Spade bag,
loss shadowed her, tapped her
on the shoulder as she strode

toward the West Side Highway
with rats and mice and the cat
from the deli swirling around her feet.
She paused, turned

just at the moment her office-structure
snapped and showered her with ash.
As quickly as a dash of salt
she stiffened into a pillar.

3:42 a.m. September 12, 2001

The sound of souls shuffling
around my bedroom woke me.
Mute sepia faces found a portal
to my Upper East Side bedroom,
packed it like the 8 a.m. F train
step in and stand clear, please.

Most of the lost were women
wearing Versace, clutching Prada bags,
stacks of papers, useless cell phones:
Current Service Unavailable.
And somehow I feel guilty:
They were all holding pens,

trying to write on my paper
but the wax of the world kept them
from forming the words till now.
It is their force driving my hand
across this page trying not
to disappoint the dead.

The Death of Little Brothers

We stood across from each other
like bullies in a playground:
sixth graders amongst a village
filled with kindergarteners.
Their existence, their size
(which I thought I'd never see)
gave me company when I
wanted none. After 42 years
of urban solitude, my Southern
exposure was witness
to their growth beginning
in 1970. People ventured to my
observation-deck to stare and
study their growth until their
steel screams rang out in '73.
I was loathe to hoist one more
monster into my horizon,
two was beyond my tolerance,
and they blocked my view
of the Harbor. I sighed down
Broadway, testing my breath
for wind enough to topple
the twins before they rose
above my Art Deco glory,
but it never seemed to work.
I tried anticipating their arrival
without malice. Newspapers blew
into my Fifth Avenue windows
and brightened my outlook.

Critics hailed me as beautiful
and them as merely two
stupid-looking parallelepipeds
soaring into my sky.
I was still named for the State,
while they, well, were born
for the Ideal World. Once they reached
their limits I began to enjoy
the new night light illuminating
lower Manhattan with hues
I had never seen before.
Anticipation stirred in me
to watch the sunlight crash
against them in the mornings.
Maybe company was just
what I needed. The twins
admired me, we developed a secret
language just for ourselves:
a visual Morse. Why, even
planes passing between us
on the way to LaGuardia
began to get the joke.
I had a bomber of my own
thrust into me the summer of '45.
I used to tell the twins
about the crash (my 79th floor).
I told them fourteen people
perished that day. Then they felt
a bomb of their own in '93.
But I never thought I would
see those who made us destroy
those young brothers of mine.

It left me big again, of course,
but melancholy now.
The City told electricians
to leave my lights burning
around the clock; everyone
needed to see I was still here.

The Renewal of 4M

When I met Carrie tonight, I had come in
the back door with grocery bags and books.
The elevator opened. We both stepped in.
She hit the button for my floor. "You new?"
I asked. "Yes, moved in today. I'm Carrie,"
she answered, "4M." I paled and swallowed
my immediate response. Do you know what happened?
She had just named Harvey's apartment.

The door-frame still gapes from the crowbar
which helped us confirm his absence. My whole
neighborhood had counted those who didn't come
home that September. Harvey happened to be the one
from my building. We were considered lucky—
the complex across the street suffered
losses I could count only in candles
blazing on the sidewalk all week long.

Candles and missing persons flyers, little
memorials littered my Upper East Side
neighborhood until October, as we all
struggled with survivor guilt—a feeling
that swallowed me whole the morning
I opened the Nation Challenged section
of *The New York Times* and discovered
Harvey's obituary in Portraits of Grief.

That same feeling lingers outside his door
each time I take the elevator. And now
here stands Carrie holding her laundry basket
and detergent, smiling and entirely innocent
of the history the broker probably "forgot"
to mention when he rented the apartment:
Charming one bedroom, southern exposure,
Upper East Side, empty six months.

How to Have A Dialogue With The Dead

Twenty thousand pieces
are logged into the city morgue,
unknown fragments:
muscle, rib, left foot—
each part haunts
the medical examiner
as he sits every night
under the white tent
the hum of the refrigerated trailers
filling his unvarying silence
while he stares into DNA puzzles
the only clues left for him
to ask over and over again
who do you belong to?

Almost Vesta

I forgot why I was even standing
on Fifth Avenue in front of Bendel's
or why I am childless
or why I hadn't any coffee
or why those people died.

The scent of the embers approached
me from the inside as I blamed
myself for snuffing out the sacred
flame when I rolled over and left
the others uncovered—exposed.

The bus stopped and I got on
behind a white haired lady
who flashed my grandmother's eyes
and that ignited me. Now the city
dwellers can again warm themselves
by the fire burning between my temples.

Revisions

I spend my time working on work
that is helping me work my way
to work that does not yet know me.

After The Second Miscarriage

I am a walking graveyard
cradling the dead I happen
to create. The dust of the
heartbeats rings my eyes
with the ceremony of burial—
so quick no spades even split
my earth. My blood fell
in neat spheres mocking me
with the shape of the world.

Growth takes place in nature
but within me life cannot evolve.
Only the idea of life occurs
and the end result defies
the true use of my body.

I continue as a false mother—
milkless and needing the needy
lives that never seem to inhabit
me. Maybe all the space within
is taken by the ghosts of my selves
and they will never allow a
newness to shine near for fear
it might reflect upon them.

III

Written From The Living

Sometimes I envy the dead.
They exist in peace, devoid
of desire and dirty socks.
No more thoughts wake them
through tiny vessels bursting
into spaces I no longer feel.
They float in the possibility
of silence broken only when
the casket lid slams shut and
then the dead open their eyes
to fabric so close to their mouths
that it may almost feel like a gag
but in that space, I can feel them
smiling.

Wien 2003

Wien 2003

I.—the beginning

Battles and rats shared the streets, Vindobona;
    streets which drank the life-blood of Marcus Aurelius,

as some still suspect. Maybe that is why the Romans left
    this city once the militant foundation was established.

Their original set of walls divided the divided.
    And that was the beginning.

The markets fed the peasants
    and the vineyards produced the Zwiegelt to

fill their mouths long before pagan tribes
    converted to stone masons devoted to erecting

places to worship a new savior,
    if only to differentiate themselves from the Turks and Islam.

And once out of the city, the Wienerwald
    created shadows, cast spells

on those who tried to flee. They were confused
    and left castles behind. The others took notes.

II.—The Muses

These Baroque facades provide the staves
On which composers pen their compositions.
Clefs become ledges for the notes arranged in waves
Of horns, keys, strings, and drums for mass and masses.
Faded inked bars of music intertwine from the minds
Of the creators around the beats of the Ringstrasse.
Beginning with Haydn, the voices chime
From the Staatsopher and from that alley on Domgasse...
Although Mozart never shared any schlag at
Demel with Beethoven, their verses harmonize
Into chords of dynamics floating around the Rathaus.
Like calls of the crows, their overtures sigh
And cluster together like their headstones in Zentralfriedhof.
The masters decompose with the ferocity of a trapped moth.

III.—Freud

The fumes of the Anschluss still smolder from those fires
ignited during the years of defeat. The blackouts continue.

The people here live alongside relics created by emperors,
which force them to circulate like serfs dwelling on crown lands.
Their buses have the audacity to puncture the Baroque gates
of the Imperial Palace with their mundane modern reality.
Everyone constantly prepares for another invasion
or starvation as they gobble bratwurst at the Wiener Wurstel.

Mozart's flute, Beethoven's symphonies, and Strauss
(the younger Johann's) waltzs loop like a soundtrack
around the archways and recall the band playing

on the decks of the Titanic as the mighty beast took its last
breath in our world only to live on, a fable in a world under
ours yet existing in the same dimension—as Vienna does with
New York.

Everything seems preserved. Yet looking closely,
you can see what was removed; Freud's couch,
swastikas, smiling at strangers. Freud left the waiting
room furniture so amateurs like me could sit here and
diagnose this civilization with collective amnesia. No
doctor waiting beyond the door with a more relevant theory.

Chocolate, coffee, wine try to fill the holes created,
if occasionally, by daggers of the silent past.

IV.— Visit from New York

The first night I slept in you, the ghosts appeared.
They took turns waking me to be sure I was not
one of them. After they had awakened me
three or four times, they went away happy.
Ghosts do not speak a universal language
and I had to remind them :
Ich spreche kein Deutsch.
Ich verstehe nicht.

The second night I slept in you, the ghosts
did not try to wake me; they understood
I could not understand them. But my presence,
as someone who could see them and
acknowledge them, made them happy.
From that night forward, we resided in

a peaceful duality, which was that of a New Yorker
walking the Vienna streets.
The bones of the land still creak under the weight
of national history—ignored by natives
but too loud to be dismissed by visitors.

The gold, the symphony, the schlag, the gray mist
cannot mask the suffering worn into your sidewalks.
The streets so unchanged that I walk along and almost expect
Mozart to bustle past, muttering something about being broke.

I walk through your streets with an intention
some might think of as soldiers marching to
another war. I search for you because I know
that somewhere within yourself you have hidden
truths I think I am capable of understanding— even translating.

Isolation

I packed up God in a little white box
and put it in a drawer before I left for work.
The coffee guy still smiled at me and added
frothed milk to my decaf and remarked
that something seemed different about me.
Maybe it's the haircut, I said.

I got on the bus and started to read the paper.
I occasionally glanced above the Metropolitan Diary
Section of *The New York Times* in an effort to see if
God had gotten out and boarded the bus with me.
Any regular day, that would be fine but not
on the day I was practicing to be an atheist.

When I reached my desk, I placed the photo of my dog
face down on the desktop—can't be too careful—
God is sneaky and could use an anagram or something.
It reminded me of when people accused the Beatles
of encoding records with backwards messages.
But that was when we allowed turn tables to slow down
or reverse time. How divine.

After I walked my dog later that evening, I creaked
around the apartment in case God had escaped the box
and was hiding under the bed. I looked. Nothing.
I ate my dinner and watched *Survivor*. Only after
I brushed my teeth and got into bed did God
turn over to talk to me.

Why did you leave me locked in that box? God asked.
I had to see what it was like, you know, being alone,
I said.
And, God said.
I'm not sure I understand the infidel ways. I answered.
Then God said, I'm glad you explored other means
of satisfaction as now I can understand your fidelity.
Turn off the light, I said.

A Visit to Combray

The lingering scent of invisible lilacs touched my nose
as I stepped off the train to attend a Saturday dinner.
I carried wrapped daffodils to the waiting table.

Francoise let me in and showed me to the little parlor
stiff with country air. A young boy came in and took my hand—
I felt his fake crushes on girls pulsing through his fingertips.

He led me to a table filled with family and flowers.
I was passed roast beef, asparagus, and potatoes with béchamel.
A pregnant servant girl brought in fresh rolls and butter.

After dinner, I asked the boy to show me the chestnut tree
in the backyard so I could see where he absorbed
Racine and Dostoevsky. No words littered the ground, yet.

I arrived too early in his life to converse with the boy about recording
memory. I strained to absorb as much imagery as I could knowing
the chrysanthemums and rain would evolve into classic

sensory details described using words as only scribes would ascend.
So I sat in the cool shade of greatness trying to forget about memory
and impressions and only enjoy the air touching my skin and this boy
chattering to me as though we might actually be acquainted.

Fragments : for Woody Allen

I went to see the man in the moon
to ask him why my faucet was leaking,
then I realized I had confused him
with Jose, the maintenance man.

But while I was there, I thought
I'd ask about the rhythm of the tides
and a woman's emotions. He said
that they were one and the same.

Emotions can pound and erode the mind,
just like waves pummeling a beach
or emotions can soothe and fixate
the mind as waves cascade

softly into the wet sand and lap
bare feet. Both need to be watched
and charted, but not involved.

Misplaced Ceremony

Well, it seems I just forgot to burn a lamb
and a dove outside the Tent of Meeting
with a priest after I gave birth to my daughter
three years ago. The Old Testament God
gets the last laugh as no attempt has helped
to further increase the size of my family.

According to Leviticus, if I cannot afford
a sacrificial lamb—I can substitute two doves or
two young pigeons. Of course one is meant
as a burnt offering and the other is to purify
me from sin. I suppose my sin is of carnal
knowledge which lead to my daughter.

Or perhaps my it is simply
the curse of being a woman.

As a New York City resident, I can certainly
attempt to locate two young pigeons. What if
I ask a pigeon its age and it lies like everyone
else on the Upper East Side? Somehow I think
the Co-Op board would have something to say
if I burned a live animal in my apartment.
Atonement sounds rather smoky.

And, I suppose, I could locate some sort of
priest to attend this ceremony with me.
Does is it count if the priest was ordained
over the internet? Is God digital?

These sacred observances—or my dismissal of them
has lead me to look up these complicated rules.
Now I am thinking about how to obey this written
word as I continue my endless search for a son.

Conversation With My Father

He talked more
about the parking garage
than he did
about the consultation
with the oncologist.

What The Dog Didn't Say

I'm trying to sleep
and you're cracking windows
and having thoughts.

Euthanasia – Weight 31-60 lbs.

I found the receipt for your
death. It was stuck in a drawer
in the kitchen under a cherry
Charms pop and next to some
taxi receipts. We took you downtown
in a taxi that Sunday. The vet
told us to come.

We had been pumping you full of drugs
and tasteless dog food that even your
hell hound tongue found too boring to eat.
Fuck it, I switched you to roast chicken,
pasta, pizza, French fries drowned in ketchup—
your favorite. It was the end—
for more than a year.

I think you enjoyed the attention
and being helped onto the bed. Although
God called to you, you kept asking
for just a couple more minutes under
our quilt.

Then the shaking started. The blood
on the floor. The urine. The total loss
of appetite. But, you took your time
letting us go. Life was still like that
chicken bone you dove for in front
of the Belaire. You knew it had been
there for three days just by sniffing—
and once you had it in your jaws—
you were not letting go.

I had to do it.

First they stopped the shaking by
injecting you with valium. You needed it
after those nights of no sleep.
Then, she administered the morphine shot.
Did you hear the yelp you made as your
breath shuddered from your lungs?

We did.

It may as well have been a scream.
We cried over your warm furry body.

And I was given this piece of paper
I now hold in my hand.

Proof. (that word sounds like a bark—*proof, proof, proof*)

You were here
and we loved you.

New Balance Due : $ 0.00

Dinner Date

The buzzer rang and the doorman sent up
Death, who brought a bottle of Merlot.
I was serving barbeque chicken, three
potato salad, and string beans.

I greeted Death at the door and took his
cloak. But there are many layers, hiding
any form from sight. The dog sniffed
around the earth on the soles of Death's feet.

My husband sliced the chicken and as we
tucked into the meal, I asked how Death's
day had gone. "Dreadful," he answered.
"All of those cadavers, day after day."

I told a lame story about realizing my shirt
was on inside out once I had boarded the bus
heading for work. "Well, at least your insides
were still inside," said Death. I grinned.

"We have chocolate mousse for dessert,"
I proclaimed. Death was quite happy and
sucked his chicken bone and drank his wine.
"Nice to have warm friends," said Death.

Death reached for my hand and held it
to his icicle cheek. I felt grateful to know him.

The Fruit of My Grandfather

I wish I knew you now that I like figs.

We will feast together on the seedy flesh in the dark wrappers.
They are so much sweeter than they look; something you had
    in common.
You tried to teach me about the secrets of figs many years ago.

The same leaves which covered Adam and Eve, cooled you
and your driveway. I was more concerned about walking
the cement rise which separated your driveway from the neighbor's.

I played for hours trying to balance myself on that straight property
    line
rather than joining you under the shade where it is said the Supreme
Buddha achieved enlightenment after mediation in another lifetime.

You would sit there, like an Italian version of Buddha, under gnarled
branches. Comfortably seated in your green and white stripped lawn
chair, you would hold your pairing knife for the flesh cutting exercises.

Now from that Promised Land, you have sent me my passion for figs.
I know that one day, we will eat them together.

To The Old Man And The Sea

Papa. You found yourself
during the u-boat hunt off the coast of Cuba.
You experienced La Mar for yourself and she
caressed you with stories. Yet you still drew
that gun to your temples only nine years later
as if she did not give you enough fulfillment—
enough plankton, enough phosphorescence for life.

You left shapes of yourself to be printed
and held again and again like waves lapping
up against the skiff. It moved towards the shore
with the corpse of you lashed to it. Your words
shine like the bones pitched clean by sharks.

How An Angel Works

Take comfort, families:
someone escorted them
to their next appointment.

I've seen him myself—
walking the corridors
of Mount Sinai in jeans,

ready to take the next
soul on the list. He checks
for weightlessness before taking you.

When you don't have the strength
or circumstances to object, he knows
you are ready to go.

But for that crowd
on Tuesday, he held
a bullhorn, shouting instructions

to his new flock.
His job: leading.

Shotgun

I understand Ernest.
Oh, I know you hate to be called that.
I think Hadley called you Hem.
I'll use the final preferred moniker of Papa.

Well, Papa.
I understand.
It was the waves.

Not the ones you describe in such detail in that
book about the sea. But, those waves that were
forced upon your brain to try to restart your life.

Those waves resembled explosion after explosion
like the landmines in those wars you loved to witness
and then detail in those periodicals for the absent.

Love started to escape you as the words started to
sputter like that car you drove around France that time
with Fitzgerald, making it to Paris one vineyard at a time.

That electricity charred your precious memory
full of plane crashes, lion hunts, and ambulances.
Waves of waves became lost waves of waves.

Oh, Papa. I know that it is hard enough
to remember how to use a semicolon
much less weave the lives of characters alive
through page after page as you did during
those wine soaked days at La Closerie de Lilas.

Finally, the narrator had to kill off its hero.
The great loss of yourself was just too much
for you—
so you had to show everyone else what it was like
to be the one to pay that death we all owe God.

The Nurses of the InBetween

My infancy still gags me as I struggle to wash the taste of the formula
from my mouth – though I was lucky to have it and be in the asylum.
The nurses wrapped me with the weight of myself, alone in a plastic bed.
Like a curse, I was a nameless paper baby, who's father had run away.
No one knew what else to do, but grant infant me a way to stay.

While the lawyers decided who I was going to be, it was the nurses
who touched me, bathed me, fed me, sang to me, changed me
when the hands of my forgotten mother were strapped to a bed
somewhere a few buildings away, never to be freed again – at least
not to hold me. No christening, no water, no forgiveness by a priest.

My mother had nurses also. Maybe some of our nurses knew both of us.
Maybe they would smoke cigarettes and drink coffee in the lounge
while they talked about the infirm mother and abandoned daughter.
Maybe they would talk about holding you down and just holding me,
during our time between who we were and who we were to be.

History Lessons

When someone gave me the tablet of myself to record upon—
I chose my chisel to carve stories into the pure, smooth stone :
the metal leg brace, birthday parties of others and my own,
battles with my brother, Homecoming photos on the lawn,
living in London, graduating from college, becoming a wife,
moving uptown to the Eastside, letting my words out of prison,
hemorrhaging on the Emergency Room floor, planning a baptism.
And I thought the hard part was trying to keep the dust of my life
from filling my eyes blind. But I knew some events happened
before I started sculpting this record, and one day I saw through
the cloud where the first tablet with my initials sat covered in dew.
To my surprise, there were experiences of mine fashioned
upon this tablet by numerous authorities – an unknown lot.
And I learned that everything I thought was my fault was not.

As a Transgression of Divine Law

after Sharon Olds

When we lived in the house at the bottom of the slippery slope of sinners,
I was a blind deaf invalid. Some would say I deserved to be that way
as I represented an error of conception between two motherless souls.
I was Shame in human form. One day, Satan sidled up to me and said,
"You know, I am going to shove you back up onto the soil away from this
sad soul muck you have shoveled your way into. But, you will have no
memory of here, though you will still live in pieces of your shame."
"Will I be someone different?" I asked.
"No," said Satan. "But you will wear a mask and I will allow your broken
legs to stand. I will shatter other parts of you instead. "
"I want you to release me," I said.
He did.
Up the slope I went
as if my body were lassoed to hell hounds barking after a rabbit.
They deftly left me naked and crying at the Social Services office in
New Haven five months into my life. The deserving came to retrieve
the new shiny me and started to swiftly wipe the sin from my face.
They swept the sin straight into the back of my brain and neatly tucked
chunks of it into my tiny serpent self which nearly burst.
They threw a baby blanket over it. But, as I grew the sin came to the
surface of myself like pimples I tried to constantly cover with scarves.
Boils of sin left rings around my uterus where Satan had grabbed me
and squeezed before I was allowed to live again as this other person
I have never met.

After Self Entombment

The world turned around to shake my hand --
I had to slither from the darkness to grasp it.
The light hurt my eyes after decades in my dirt.

The hand of the world was warm and wet
with the breath of the souls inhabiting it.
My pale boney digits were lost, yet gripped.

I felt myself rising full of hope and unrest.
The blanket of my grief slipped off of me and
past my feet as I was lifted up past my youth –

I could see a me that was worthy of this release.
I saw, for the first time, what the world wanted to know.
And it was - surprisingly - good.

Appreciation Page

I would like to extend a special thanks to my longtime teacher and mentor, Molly Peacock. Thank you, thank you, thank you.

I would like to thank the School of the Arts at Columbia University, particularly the great Richard Howard and Lucie Brock-Broido as well as all of the other fabulous teachers and students there. Thank you to the 92nd Street Y for their support with readings and classes for poets. Also, I would like to extend my appreciation for my past teachers the poets Phillis Levin, Donna Masini, and Mary Stewart Hammond. Thank you to the Cathedral of St. John the Divine in Manhattan for its continued annual Maundy Thursday reading of Dante's Inferno. I am honored to be included.

Thank you for the stimulating conversation – Susan Bachelder. Thank you to my mother, Dr. Angela Hill and the late Donald Hill – who guided me every step of the way. Thank you to my brother Robert Hill and his family. Thank you to many I work with in the advertising/film community particularly Amanda Rosenberg, Becky Razzell, Mary Knox, Lori & Kelsey Youmans, Claire Worch, Amy Jones (for throwing my Columbia graduation party), everyone at the Association of Independent Commercial Producers. Thank you also to Louise Devlin and Anjali Hasija. Thanks to everyone I was with on 9/11, and everyone who I work with on a daily basis. And, of course, my husband Wayne Braino Bjerke.

Lastly, I cannot be who I am without New York City. It is truly the greatest city in the world and I find it thrilling to be here everyday. NYC you make me do my work because creativity is contagious. Never sleep.

Made in the USA
Middletown, DE
09 January 2016